SO WHAT IS PATRIOTISM ANYWAY?

JOHN LAMACHIA

T 29010

So what is patriotism anyway?

the rosen publishing group / rosen central

new york

Published in 2000 by The Rosen Publishing Group, Inc.
29 East 21st Street, New York, NY 10010

First Edition

LaMachia, John
    So what is patriotism anyway? / John LaMachia.
        p. cm. — (A Student's Guide to American civics)
    Includes bibliographical references and index.
    Summary: Examines the concept of patriotism, its many sym-
bols, and how Americans, past and present, have proven themselves to be patriots.
    ISBN 0-8239-3098-X
    1. Patriotism—United States Juvenile literature.
[1. Patriotism.] I. Title.   II. Series.
JK1759.L23   1999
323.6'5—dc21   99-32690
                                                        CIP

Manufactured in the United States of America

CONTENTS

INTRODUCTION
WHAT IS A DEMOCRACY?

The government of the United States is a democracy. A democracy is a government of the people, by the people, and for the people. In a democracy, every citizen is entitled to certain rights and freedoms. A citizen is a person who was born in, or who has chosen to become a member of, a particular country. An American citizen's rights and freedoms are guaranteed by the Bill of Rights. The Bill of Rights is the first ten amendments to the U.S. Constitution. A constitution states the powers of a country's government and the rights of its citizens. The First Amendment of the U.S. Constitution, for example, guarantees that citizens have freedom of speech, freedom of the press, freedom to practice the religion of their choice, and the right to assemble peacefully.

The President, Congress, governors, mayors, and sheriffs are all important people in our democratic government. They make and enforce laws that help protect us, our rights, and our freedoms. You can help ensure these rights and freedoms by being a good citizen. In this book, we will discuss one aspect of being a good citizen: patriotism.

The Bill of Rights

Congress of the United States,
begun and held at the City of New-York,
on Wednesday the fourth of March one thousand seven hundred and eighty nine.

so what is patriotism anyway?

Patriotism—Love of Country

Patriotism means having a strong love for and pride in your country. People have such strong feelings for their country because it is where they live. Patriotism is also a desire to support your country and defend its honor. Patriots show their love of country by making it a better place to live. They obey their country's laws and show respect for their country. They are involved in

Thomas Jefferson

what their government is doing. Patriots also honor their country by setting a good example for others to follow.

One of the greatest American patriots was Thomas Jefferson. Jefferson was a wealthy, educated landowner who led a privileged life as a lawyer and legislator. Yet Jefferson had such a strong love for this country, he risked everything for it—his wealth, his position in society, and even his life. When Jefferson was 33 years old, he decided to take action to show his commitment to American independence. On July 4, 1776,

The Declaration of Independence and the Liberty Bell

Jefferson drafted, and signed with other patriots, the Declaration of Independence. This document stated that the American colonies intended to break away from England, whose kings had ruled over them for

Thomas Jefferson and many other leaders signed the Declaration of Independence.

more than a century. Had Jefferson been captured by the British, the act of writing the Declaration of Independence would have cost him his life.

Jefferson strongly believed that the main ideas behind British "subjectship" were wrong. A subject is a person who owes his or her allegiance, or loyalty, to a king. Jefferson believed that no leader has the right to rule just because he or she is born into royalty. He felt that people had the right to say how they wanted to be governed. He believed no one was born a better person than anyone else. "All men," Jefferson wrote in the Declaration of Independence, "are created equal."

ALL MEN ARE CREATED EQUAL

A government, Jefferson thought, should be chosen by the people being governed, and it should work to protect and serve them. "Kings are the servants of their people, not their owners," he wrote. Thomas Jefferson was one of the inventors of a new kind of government: a democracy.

As the third president of the United States, Jefferson continued to support democratic ideas. He served two terms, from 1801 to 1809. He died on July 4, 1826, fifty years to the day after signing the Declaration of Independence. Thanks to Jefferson, one of the greatest patriots in U.S. history, American citizens are able to enjoy the Declaration's promise of "Life, Liberty and the pursuit of Happiness."

so what is patriotism anyway?

How Do You Become a Patriot?

CHAPTER TWO

Children are not born with a love of their country. They are too young to understand what it means to be from a particular country. They know only about a very small world—their home. To children, home is a place where everything is safe and familiar. From a very young age, children understand that they belong in this group called a family.

In a family, children learn about their heritage—who they are and where they are from. They learn family traditions and discover things that make their families unique. Children also learn from their families about love and devotion. They are taught what it means to care for somebody. Children discover that members of a family will help and support one another. They learn to feel pride in themselves and in their families.

In places such as schools and houses of worship, children widen the circle of people who are important to them. They develop relationships with other children. They discover that friendships also involve devotion and loyalty. They learn that friends, like family members, stand by one another.

Learning family traditions, such as recipes, helps you understand what makes your family unique.

This feeling that you will support a person or a group of people no matter what happens is called loyalty. You probably feel loyalty to your family and friends. You may feel a sense of loyalty to your school, too. This feeling of school loyalty is often called school "spirit."

If you've ever played a team sport or rooted for a particular team, you have probably felt this kind of loyalty, called team spirit. When you wear a team uniform, you are saying that you're a part of something larger than yourself. You feel pride in your team's uniform and name. You try to do your best because other people are depending on you. You don't give up on your team, even if it's losing. You feel pride in your teammates and their accomplishments.

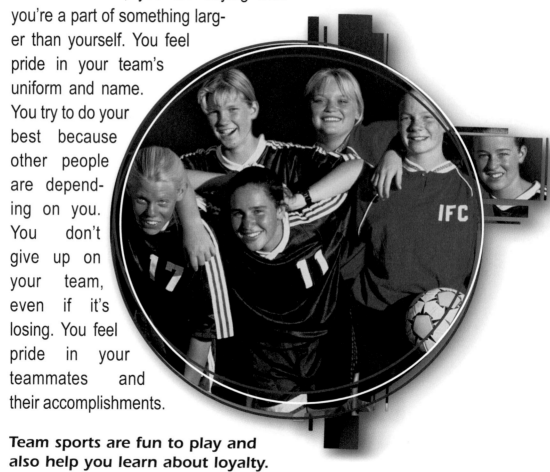

Team sports are fun to play and also help you learn about loyalty.

Patriotism is another kind of loyalty—loyalty to a country. Many people call their country a fatherland, a motherland, or a homeland. Even the word "patriot" comes from the Latin word *pater*, which means "father." This strong sense of love and devotion to one's fatherland can be shown in many ways.

In many towns and cities, people march with the American flag in Fourth of July parades.

so what is patriotism anyway?

Patriotic Symbols

You can show loyalty and devotion to your country by singing your country's national anthem or displaying its flag. In America, the national anthem is played before most sports games. Many American citizens proudly hang U.S. flags to celebrate national holidays, such as Flag Day and the Fourth of July. Another way to demonstrate your loyalty to America is by saying the Pledge of Allegiance in school each morning. When people hear their national song, see their country's flag, or recite their country's pledge, they feel patriotic about their country.

THE PLEDGE OF ALLEGIANCE

The Pledge of Allegiance is an oath in which American citizens promise to support their country. The pledge of allegiance is: "I pledge allegiance to the flag of the United States of America and to the Republic for which it stands, one nation under God, indivisible, with liberty and justice for all."

Reciting the Pledge of Allegiance and singing the national anthem are two ways you can show your patriotism.

CHAPTER THREE

The Pledge of Allegiance

Francis Bellamy, a Baptist minister, wrote the original Pledge of Allegiance in August 1892. His original pledge was: "I pledge allegiance to my flag and the Republic for which it stands; one nation indivisible, with liberty and justice for all." In 1923 and 1924 the National Flag Conference changed "my flag" to "the flag of the United States of America." In 1954 Congress added the words "under God" to the pledge.

NATIONAL ANTHEMS

Most countries have a special patriotic song called a national anthem. A national anthem celebrates and praises a country and expresses patriotic feelings for it. Patriotic people usually stand up when they sing their national anthem. Even if they do not sing, they stand quietly while the song plays.

The American national anthem is "The Star-Spangled Banner." It was written by a lawyer, Francis Scott Key, during the War of 1812 between the United States and England. Key was awaiting the end of a battle at Fort McHenry in Baltimore, Maryland, to return home to Washington, DC. At dawn, he looked through a telescope to see whether the fort had been lost to the British. There he saw the American flag flying in victory. Key was so inspired that he grabbed the first thing he could find—the back of an envelope he had in his pocket—and began writing. Within a few days, Key had finished his poem. He had it printed and distributed. It was soon put to the melody of the British song "To Anacreon in Heaven." The new song and the flag that inspired it became known as "The Star-

Spangled Banner." In 1931 Congress declared "The Star-Spangled Banner" the national anthem of the United States.

The Star-Spangled Banner

Oh, say can you see by the dawn's
   early light
What so proudly we hail'd at the
   twilight's last gleaming,
Whose broad stripes and bright
   stars through the perilous fight
O'er the ramparts we watch'd
   were so gallantly streaming?
And the rockets' red glare, the
   bombs bursting in air,
Gave proof through the night that
   our flag was still there.
Oh, say does that star-spangled
   banner yet wave
O'er the land of the free and the
   home of the brave?

FLAGS

Every country has a flag. A flag may seem like just a piece of colorful cloth, but it is very important to the citizens of a country. People usually stand up when their flag goes by in a parade. They may place their hands over their hearts or even salute as their flag is raised. Soldiers carry their country's flag into battle. Mountain climbers often bring their country's flag on their treks. When the climbers reach the top of a mountain, they fly their country's flag from a pole. Explorers do the same when they discover new lands. American astronauts were the first space explorers to walk on the moon's surface. People all over the world watched as they flew the U.S. flag on the moon.

In 1969, Americans became the first people to walk on the moon.

The American Flag

On June 14, 1777, America's government at the time, the Continental Congress, declared that "the flag of the United States be thirteen stripes, alternate red and white; [and] that the union be thirteen stars, white in a blue field, representing a new constellation."

The number of stripes and stars represented the thirteen original states: Delaware, Pennsylvania, New Jersey, Georgia, Connecticut, Massachusetts, Maryland, South Carolina, New Hampshire, Virginia, New York, North Carolina, and Rhode Island. By 1795 two more stripes and stars were added for the two new states, Vermont and Kentucky.

By 1818 it was apparent that the number of states was going to keep growing. It was decided to return to the original flag with thirteen stripes and add stars as states joined the union. The most recent state to join the United States was Hawaii, in 1959. The total number of states, and of stars on the flag, is fifty.

OTHER SYMBOLS OF PATRIOTISM

The Statue of Liberty is one of America's most powerful patriotic symbols, representing the freedom that is found in the United States. The Statue of Liberty is a giant statue of a woman that stands in New York

City Harbor. The statue stands 151 feet high (305 feet, including its pedestal) and weighs 225 tons. "Lady Liberty," as the statue is also known, holds a torch high over her head. For many years, when people came by boat to the United States from other countries, the statue was the first thing they saw. Lady Liberty seemed to welcome them to their new home—America. She was a symbol of the freedom they hoped to find in their new land.

Some symbols change their meaning over time. In Paris, France, there stands a building called the Bastille. The Bastille was once a prison that stood as a symbol of royal oppression over the people of France. In 1787 the French people went to war against their king in an uprising called the French Revolution. The people of France wanted to run their country themselves, just as the Americans were doing. On July 14, 1789, a mob of people took over the Bastille and freed the prisoners held there. The Bastille was no longer a symbol of oppression. Instead, it became a symbol of freedom from the king. Today, the French celebrate their independence day, Bastille Day, on July 14.

When the French people stormed the Bastille, it held only seven prisoners.

The meaning of other country's symbols may be less clear. China's Great Wall is one such example. Construction of the Great Wall took more than one thousand years—beginning in 403 BC and lasting until AD 618. The wall was built to protect China against enemies. It now stretches for nearly 4,000 miles along China's border. The Great Wall is so large that it can even be seen from the moon. To many Chinese people, the Great Wall is a symbol of China's strength. It signifies that China is a proud country that doesn't need help from other countries. Some people in China, however, would like to see the Great Wall torn down. These people believe that China does need to open its borders and accept help from other countries.

The Great Wall of China in winter

so what is patriotism anyway?

CHAPTER FOUR

GREAT PATRIOTS

"Ask not what your country can do for you; ask what you can do for your country," said John F. Kennedy, the thirty-fifth president of the United States. Kennedy meant that a true patriot gives something back to his or her community. The people mentioned here are just a few of the many patriots that have helped make and keep the United States democratic.

GEORGE WASHINGTON

George Washington was a famous patriot of the American Revolution. He was commander of the American army during the Revolutionary War, in which the American colonies broke away from England. After the colonies won the war, George Washington became the first president of a new country, the United States. Washington came to be known as "the father of his country." A man who spoke at George Washington's funeral said Washington

George Washington

was "first in war, first in peace, and first in the hearts of his countrymen." More than 200 years after George Washington died, people in the United States still remember him as one of the nation's greatest patriots.

MOLLY PITCHER

By 1778 the American Revolution had been going on for three long years. Thousands of people had died, and there seemed to be no end in sight to the war. Some women chose to help their country by following their husbands into battle. A woman called Molly Pitcher was one of these women. During the Battle of Monmoth in New Jersey, Molly Pitcher fetched water for the hot, tired soldiers. Dodging bullets and cannonballs, she ran back and forth to a creek, hauling water for the men. When her husband passed out from exhaustion, Pitcher took his place at the cannon and kept the big gun firing.

Molly Pitcher is just one of the brave, patriotic women who took part in the fight for their country during the American Revolution.

Molly Pitcher at the Battle of Monmoth

NATHAN HALE

During the American Revolution, the British captured a twenty-one-year-old lieutenant in the U.S. Continental army, Nathan Hale. Hale refused to tell British soldiers what he knew about the American army's battle strategies. He told his captors, "Nothing could make me turn traitor to my country." Hale meant that nothing the British could do would make him betray America. The penalty for not turning over informa-

A British soldier prepares to hang Nathan Hale.

tion to the British was death. As a British soldier put a noose around Hale's neck, Hale said, "I regret that I have but one life to lose for my country."

"I REGRET THAT I HAVE BUT ONE LIFE TO LOSE FOR MY COUNTRY"

Hale's last words are famous. They are often used as an example of the devotion a patriot can have for his country.

SOJOURNER TRUTH

Born Isabella Baumfree in 1797, Sojourner Truth lived as a slave until 1827, when slavery was abolished in New York State. Believing she had received a message from God, Isabella renamed herself Sojourner Truth and became a full-time preacher. She traveled to camps, churches, and towns across the country speaking about her life. She was a powerful preacher and singer. She argued for abolishing slavery entirely and campaigned for equal rights for women. Sojourner Truth is considered one of the first advocates of women's rights. In 1851 she gave a famous speech called "Ain't I A Woman?" at a women's rights convention. After the Civil War, when slavery was finally abolished throughout the country, Truth tried to get Congress to distribute land to former slaves. Congress refused. She was, however, successful in the fight to integrate streetcars.

Sojourner Truth

Sojourner Truth was honored on a U.S. commemorative postage stamp in 1986. In 1995 the Mars Pathfinder microrover, a vehicle that was part of the space mission, was named in her honor. As a patriot and citizen, Truth exercised her right to speak up for what she believed.

SAMANTHA SMITH

In 1982 ten-year-old Samantha Smith of Manchester, Maine, was worried about the possibility of a nuclear war between the United States and Russia, formerly known as the Soviet Union, or USSR. Smith wrote a letter to Yuri Andropov, then a high-ranking official of the Communist party of the USSR. She told Andropov how scared she felt and asked him if he truly wanted war between their countries. Smith took the safety of her country very seriously.

Samantha Smith on a Soviet stamp

Andropov wrote back and invited Smith to visit the Soviet Union as his guest. He wanted her to meet the people of the Soviet Union and see for herself what they were like. Smith and her parents flew to the Soviet Union and spent two weeks touring the country and spreading good-will. The Soviet people were so impressed that they created a stamp in her honor. Many Americans consider this little girl a great patriot.

NATO FORCES

The North Atlantic Treaty was signed in Washington, DC, on April 4, 1949, in response to the threat of communism. It created an alliance called the North Atlantic Treaty Organization (NATO), made up of twelve nations committed to one another's defense. Today, nineteen countries are members of NATO, including the United Kingdom, the

(clockwise from top right)
NATO bombing in Belgrade;
a young Kosovar refugee;
the aftermath of a NATO attack

The signing of the North
Atlantic Peace Treaty
agreement in 1949 created
the NATO alliance.

Czech Republic, France, Germany, Canada, and the United States. Each country contributes armed forces and weapons to any action designated by NATO. These actions include protecting member countries and establishing peace in other countries. One of the places where NATO decided to act was Kosovo.

Kosovo is a province of Serbia, a country in Europe. Since 1998, ethnic Albanians (people who were born in another country but are Albanian by heritage) have been killed or forced to leave Kosovo. Ethnic Albanians make up 90 percent of the population of the country; the Serbians make up only 10 percent. Ethnic Albanians want Kosovo to become a country independent from Serbia. The Serbians, however, believe that Kosovo is an important part of their history and their country. They would rather get rid of the ethnic Albanians than allow Kosovo to become independent. The Serbians have killed thousands of ethnic Albanians and forced hundreds of thousands of others to flee their homeland.

NATO began a bombing campaign on March 24, 1999, in response to the Serbian attacks on ethnic Albanians. Soon after, NATO began bombing military targets in nearby Belgrade, Yugoslavia. NATO took these actions to prevent the killing or evicting of any more ethnic Albanians. American soldiers were a part of that effort. As patriots, the soldiers risked their lives in the name of America—a country that works to keep peace around the world.

CHAPTER FIVE

PATRIOT AND PROTESTER

There are times when, to be a patriot, a person must object to what his or her government is doing. To some, it may seem like these protesters are betraying their country. However, one of the most important things a patriot can do is to protest unfair or unjust laws in the hope that they will be changed.

WOMEN'S RIGHT TO VOTE

One of the roles of a patriot is to improve the conditions in his or her country. Before 1920 women were not allowed to vote in the United States. In the mid-1860s, women began to fight for this right. Someone who fights for the right to vote is called a suffragist. Elizabeth Cady Stanton, Susan B. Anthony, and Lucy Stone were pioneer suffragists in the fight for a woman's right to vote.

Working as a team, Stone, Stanton, and Anthony traveled across the country speaking at meetings and passing out pamphlets about the issue. They started an organization called the National Woman Suffrage Association. The women organized rallies and marches. They published articles calling for equal rights for women. In 1872 and again in 1873, Susan B. Anthony tried to vote in New York elections. Both times she

Susan B. Anthony

Elizabeth Cady Stanton

Lucy Stone

was arrested for her efforts. This did not stop her, Stanton, or Stone from continuing their fight. Finally, in 1920, Congress passed the 19th Amendment to the Constitution, giving women the right to vote.

Stanton, Anthony, and Stone, along with thousands of other women, opposed their government to win the fight for the right to vote. Their dedication to the woman's suffrage movement shows that they were true patriots.

WAR PROTESTERS

The Vietnam War, which began in the mid-1960s, was one that many Americans did not think should be fought. Many people, including college students, professors, and some government officials, believed the war was wrong and was not winnable. They believed that sending more men to Vietnam meant sending them to die for an unworthy cause.

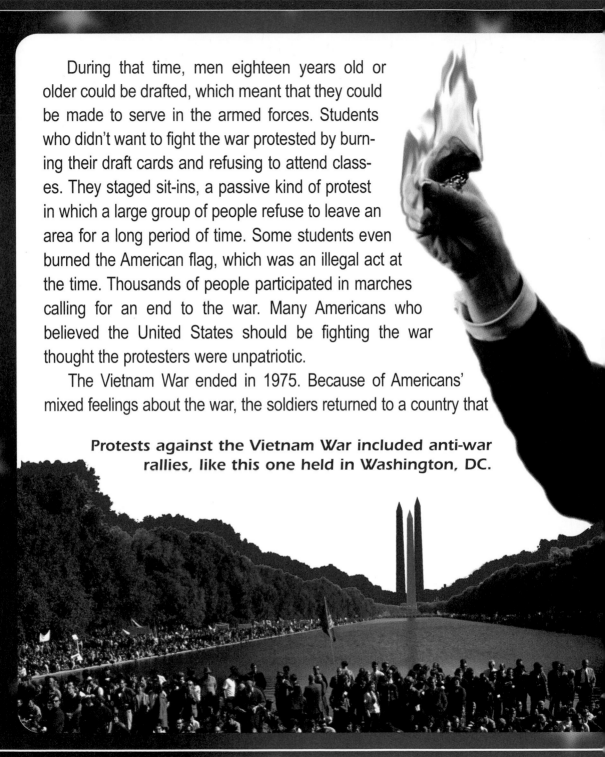

During that time, men eighteen years old or older could be drafted, which meant that they could be made to serve in the armed forces. Students who didn't want to fight the war protested by burning their draft cards and refusing to attend classes. They staged sit-ins, a passive kind of protest in which a large group of people refuse to leave an area for a long period of time. Some students even burned the American flag, which was an illegal act at the time. Thousands of people participated in marches calling for an end to the war. Many Americans who believed the United States should be fighting the war thought the protesters were unpatriotic.

The Vietnam War ended in 1975. Because of Americans' mixed feelings about the war, the soldiers returned to a country that

Protests against the Vietnam War included anti-war rallies, like this one held in Washington, DC.

was angry with them. The soldiers had done their patriotic duty by fighting a war their country had told them to fight. Yet many members of the public did not recognize this.

Both groups of people, the soldiers and the protesters, were patriots. The soldiers did their duty as citizens by serving in the armed forces. The protesters also did their duty as citizens by protesting a government action they did not agree with.

CIVIL DISOBEDIENCE

The U.S. Constitution states that the law must protect the safety, security, and rights of all people equally. Laws that fail to provide equal protection to all of a nation's citizens are unjust. To protest unjust laws, some people take part in a form of nonviolent protest called civil disobedience. Civil disobedience is the practice of disobeying the government and breaking the law on purpose to make a point. The term comes from

Henry David Thoreau

the famous 1849 essay "Civil Disobedience" by philosopher and author Henry David Thoreau.

On March 26, 1999, Reverend Jesse Jackson, former New York Mayor David Dinkins, and 215 other people were arrested for protesting the killing of Amadou Diallo by New York City police. They were also protesting what they believed was an increase in police brutality. The demonstrators blocked the entrance of police headquarters in the hope of being arrested. These patriotic citizens practiced civil disobedience because they believed that these issues were important enough to make them break the law.

so what is patriotism anyway?

Patriotism Taken Too Far

Being a patriot does not mean blindly following the leaders of your country. As a patriot, your job is to think, not just follow. You already have strong feelings about right and wrong. When you are asked to do something that you know is wrong, an alarm goes off inside your head. Listen to that alarm. It's up to you as a citizen and patriot to let your leaders know when you feel they are asking you to do something wrong.

When patriotism is taken to an extreme, when it no longer supports things that are good or right, it is called "nationalism." Nationalism happens when a country tries to pursue its own interests at the expense of other countries. A nationalist is someone who values his or her country above all other countries.

NAZI GERMANY

Adolph Hitler was a German nationalist who thought that his country and culture were better than other countries and cultures. He also was obsessed with power, and with getting rid of people he did not like or understand. "Heil Hitler!" was what many German people cried during World War II to show that they believed in their Nazi leader. Some

Nazi leader Adolph Hitler and a member of the Hitler Youth

of the people who said these words were children.

Many German children joined the Hitler Youth, an organization in which young Germans were taught Nazi ideas. One of the things they learned was to report anyone who disagreed with Hitler's beliefs or spoke out against their leader. Some children even reported their own parents to the police. The children's parents were sometimes killed or put in concentration camps. Concentration camps were prisons where people were worked, starved, or put to death.

The children of the Hitler Youth thought of themselves as patriots. They did what their leader asked them to do. Would they have followed their leader if they had known that he was wrong?

KAMIKAZE PILOTS

Halfway across the world, Japanese soldiers were killing themselves in the name of patriotism. These men flew planes for Japan during World War II and were known as kamikaze pilots. They had been taught that it was an honor to die for Japan. The job of a kamikaze pilot was to crash his plane into an enemy ship. He would sacrifice his own life, but could kill hundreds of his enemies in the process. Each kamikaze pilot wanted a chance to die that way.

In battle, many soldiers are willing to die for their country. Yet they usually do not do so on purpose. The kamikaze pilots of Japan died in the name of patriotism. They were heroes to many Japanese people. But were they true patriots?

People have committed crimes and even killed in the name of patriotism. You might think, "I would never do something like that!" and you probably wouldn't. People who have committed terrible acts in the name of patriotism probably thought they never would do these things either. To be a good citizen, it is important to think about what your government asks you to do. It is also important to listen to your own sense of right and wrong.

Kamikaze pilots sacrificed their lives for Japan during World War II.

so what is patriotism anyway?

WHAT YOU CAN DO

You don't have to be a famous leader or a soldier or risk your life to be a patriot. You don't even have to be an adult. All you have to do is be willing to love and support your country. Here are some ways you can show that you are a patriot.

RESPECT YOUR COUNTRY

There are many ways to show that you respect your country. You can stand up when the national anthem is played or when the flag goes by in a parade. You can say the Pledge of Allegiance.

Respecting your country means respecting the land as well. A good way to show you care for America and its environment is by recycling, conserving water, and not littering.

Another way you can show respect for your country is by representing it well. If you travel to another country, the people you meet there usually know what country you are from. They decide how they feel about your country by the way you act. If you are disrespectful, they may believe that most people from the United States are rude and ill-mannered. If you are polite, you will be giving them a good impression of America.

Recycling is a good way to show respect for your country.

DO YOUR DUTIES AS A CITIZEN

There are many ways to be a good citizen. You can obey the laws of a country. You can speak up about issues that you don't agree with. You can treat people fairly. You can help out in your community by volunteering at a soup kitchen or by cleaning up the neighborhood park. As an adult, you can serve on a jury, vote, and serve in the armed forces if the government asks you to.

SHOW SUPPORT FOR YOUR COUNTRY

If someone says negative things about the United States, speak up. As a patriotic American citizen, it is your duty to tell others how you feel about your country. Give them examples of positive things that Americans have accomplished. Take pride in the country that created the first modern democratic government.

HELP NEW U.S. CITIZENS

Most immigrants have a special place in their hearts for their homelands and for the people they left behind. They often continue to speak their native language at home, even if they have learned the language of their new country. Many immigrant families take great care to teach their children about the customs and traditions of their native country. Children of immigrants may grow up feeling as if they belong to two nations, their old one and their new one.

If you are a native-born citizen of the United States, you can help new citizens by reaching out to them. One way is to show respect for their traditions while teaching them about American customs. You can work

BECOMING A U.S. CITIZEN

There are two ways to become a U.S. citizen. The first is to be born in the United States. The second is to move to the United States from another country and choose to become an American.

When people leave the country where they were born, they emigrate from that country. People who are new to a country are called immigrants. In America, immigrants must learn about the United States and pass a test before they can become citizens. They must take an oath of allegiance to the United States and promise to honor the American flag. They also must give up being a citizen of their homeland.

Once immigrants do become citizens, they share all the rights and responsibilities that other U.S. citizens have. They promise to pay taxes, vote in elections, and serve in the armed forces if necessary, as well as fulfill all the other duties of citizenship. This includes being patriotic toward the United States. The challenge for many new U.S. citizens is maintaining the traditions of their old country while adapting to their new country.

together with new citizens to make the United States a better place for everyone.

CHOOSE LEADERS WISELY

When it's your turn to vote for representatives in the government, be sure you make informed decisions. Leaders should care about the country as much as you do. If you disagree with what your leaders are doing, you should speak out. You can write an editorial to your local newspaper. You can call or write your representative, or speak up at a town meeting. If you and your parents disagree with a policy at your school, you have the right to say so at the next school board meeting. You can vote against a leader who is not doing a good job. You may even choose to become a leader yourself one day. You can start by running for your school's student government.

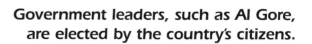

Government leaders, such as Al Gore, are elected by the country's citizens.

Remember, the United States is your home. Show respect for your country, fulfill your duties as a citizen, support your country, and participate in choosing your leaders. It is up to you to make your country a great place to live by being the best citizen and patriot you can be.

GLOSSARY

advocate A person who publicly supports something.

allegiance Devotion to something or someone.

amendment A change to something.

anthem A patriotic song.

bill of rights A document that lists and protects the individual rights of people.

citizen A person who by birth or choice is a member of a nation.

civil disobedience Disobeying the government and breaking the law through nonviolent means to protest an issue.

constitution A document stating the powers of a country's government and the rights of its citizens.

democracy A government that is run by the people who live under it.

emigrate To leave one's own country to settle in another.

immigrant A person who comes into a foreign country to live.

loyalty A feeling or the behavior of being true and faithful to something or someone.

nationalism Valuing and promoting your country above all other countries.

nationalist A person who values and promotes his or her country over all other countries.

patriot A person who loves his or her country and gives it support.

patriotism Love and loyal support of one's country.

protest A statement or act in which a person or group objects strongly to something.

subject A person who owes his or her loyalty to a king or queen.

suffragist A person who fights for the right to vote.

volunteer To offer one's services for free.

For Further Reading

Bratman, Fred. *Becoming a Citizen: Adopting A New Home* (Good Citizenship Library). Austin, TX: Steck-Vaughn Company, 1993.

Denenberg, Barry. *Voices from Vietnam.* New York: Scholastic Paperback, 1997.

Haines, Frances S. *Rights and Responsibilities: Using Your Freedom.* (Good Citizenship Library). Austin, TX: Steck-Vaughn Company, 1993.

Heyes, Eileen. *Children of the Swastika: The Hitler Youth.* Brookfield, CT: Millbrook Press, 1993.

Kiwark, Barbara. *They Shall Be Heard: The Story of Susan B. Anthony and Elizabeth Cady Stanton* (Stories of America). Austin, TX: Raintree/Steck-Vaughn, 1996.

Reit, Seymour. *Guns for General Washington: A Story of the American Revolution* (Great Episodes). New York: Harcourt Brace, 1992.

Stevenson, Augusta. *Molly Pitcher, Young Patriot.* New York: Alladin Paperbacks, 1986.

Strom, Yale. *Quilted Landscapes: Conversations with Young Immigrants.* New York: Simon & Schuster, 1996.

Whalin, Terry. *Sojourner Truth: American Abolitionist* (Heroes of the Faith). New York: Chelsea House Publishing, 1998.

Whitman, Sylvia. *Uncle Sam Wants You: Military Men and Women of World War II.* Miinneapolis, MN: Lerner Publications Company, 1993.

RESOURCES

DO SOMETHING
423 West 55th Street
8th Floor
New York, NY 10019
(212) 523-1175
Web site:
http://www.dosomething.org/

HABITAT FOR HUMANITY
Campus Chapters and Youth
Programs Department
121 Habitat Street
Americus, GA 31709
(912) 924-6935
Web site: http://www.habitat.org/

KIDS CARE CLUBS
P.O. Box 1083
New Canaan, CT 06840
(203) 972-6601
Web site: http://kidscare.org/

YOUTH IN ACTION NETWORK
Web site:
http://www.mightymedia.com/act/

BOY SCOUTS OF AMERICA
Contact the Boy Scouts of
America council in your area.
Web site:
http://www.bsa.scouting.org/

GIRL SCOUTS OF AMERICA
Contact the Girl Scouts of
America council in your area.
Web site:
http://www.girlscouts.org/

INDEX

A

allegiance, 9, 42
amendments, 4, 31
American Revolution, the (The Revolutionary War), 23, 24, 25
Andropov, Yuri, 27
Anthony, Susan B., 30, 31
armed forces, 32, 33, 40, 42

B

Bellamy, Francis, 16
Bill of Rights, the, 4

C

Cady Stanton, Elizabeth, 30, 31
citizen, 4, 9, 15, 19, 33, 35, 37, 40, 42, 43
civil disobedience, 33
Civil War, the, 26
community, 23, 40
Congress, U.S., 4, 16, 18, 26, 31
Constitution, U.S., 4, 31, 33
Continental Congress, 19
culture, 35
customs, 43

D

Declaration of Independence, the, 8, 9
democracy, 4, 9, 40
demonstrators, 33
Diallo, Amadou, 33
Dinkins, David, 33

E

England, 8, 17, 23
equal rights, 26, 30

F

flag, 15, 16, 17, 19, 20, 32, 39, 42
Flag Day, 15
Fourth of July, 15
freedom, 4, 20, 21
French Revolution, the, 21

G

government, 4, 7, 9, 19, 30, 31, 33, 37, 40

H

Hale, Nathan, 25
heritage, 11, 29

ABOUT THE AUTHOR
John LaMachia is a freelance writer with an avid interest in U.S. history and government. He lives in Upstate New York.

PHOTO CREDITS
Cover photo © TonyStone Images; pp. 5, 7, 17, 25, 32, 33 © CORBIS/Bettman; p. 6 © TonyStone/Reza Estakhrian; pp. 8, 16 © A/P Wide World Photos; p. 10 © TonyStone/Walter Hodges; p. 12 © TonyStone/Bob Terrez; p. 13 © TonyStone/Ron Sherman; p. 14 © TonyStone/Donna Day; p. 14 © A/P Wide World/Mark Lennihan; p. 19 © TonyStone/World Perspectives; p. 20 © CORBIS/Gail Mooney; p. 21 © CORBIS/Gianni Dagli Orti; p. 22 © TonyStone/ Jerry Alexander; p. 23 © CORBIS/Museum of the City of New York; pp. 24, 26, 28, 31 © Archive Photos; p. 27 © Reuters/Lev Nosov/Archive; p. 28 © Reuters/EMIL VAS/Archive; p. 28 © CORBIS/AFP; pp. 31, 34, 40 © CORBIS; p. 32 © CORBIS/Leif Skoogfors; pp. 36, 37 © CORBIS/Hulton-Deutsch Collection; p. 38 © TonyStone/David Wolff.

Design and Layout
Kim M. Sonsky

Consulting Editors
Mark Beyer and Jennifer Ceaser